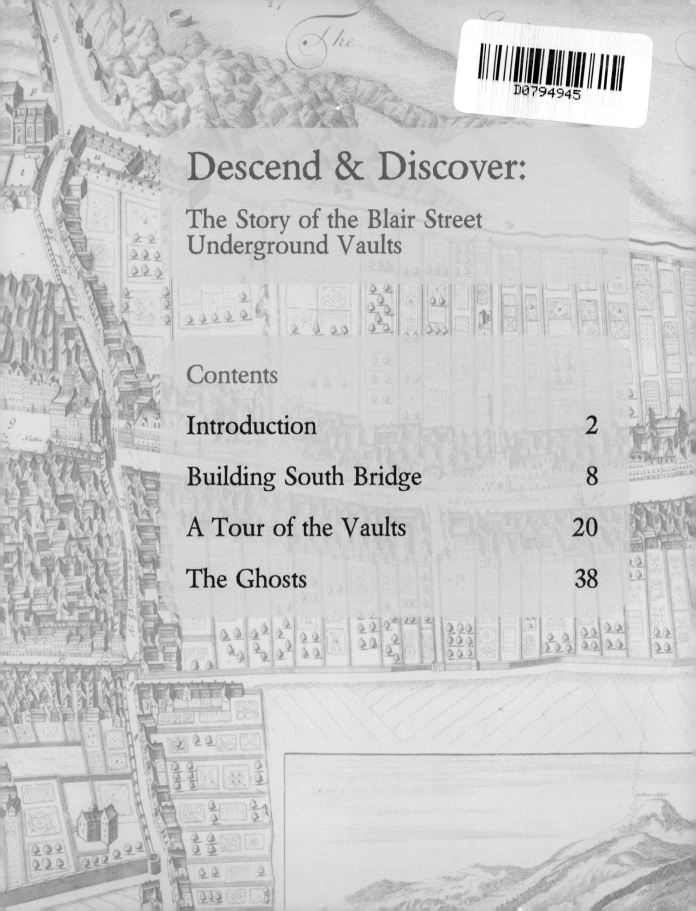

Descend & Discover:

The Story of the Blair Street Underground Vaults

Contents

Introduction

The South Bridge, linking the Royal Mile with Edinburgh's Southside, has stood for over 200 years, since the 1780s.

Beneath the shops and the road stand 19 enormous arches which support the bridge.

In the arches are vaulted chambers, linked by a honeycomb of passageways. Abandoned in the mid 1800s, most lay deserted for over a hundred years till they were rediscovered in the 1980s. Mercat Tours has been guiding visitors round the vaults since 1996.

Welcome to the Blair Street Vaults.

If you have this book in your hand, the chances are you have just enjoyed a Mercat historical or ghostly tour of Blair Street Vaults. Perhaps you would like

- a souvenir of your experience

- to retrace your steps round the vaults

- more information about different aspects of the bridge and vaults

- exclusive illustrations

{ This book is a personal guide which takes you on a tour from the comfort of your sofa. Descend and discover as you turn the page . . . }

Vaulted chambers are linked by a honeycomb of passageways.

The Mercat Cross

Our story of Blair Street Vaults starts, as do all Mercat tours, at the Mercat Cross on the High Street in the Royal Mile. This was where merchants came to trade and locals came to get the news. Public proclamations are still made from the balcony.

Visitors follow another old custom in coming to the Cross to find a guide. In the 1700s they would hire a 'caddie', a guide who would carry their bags, take them to where they wanted to go and tell them about Edinburgh.

Today visitors have to carry their own bags and go on foot, not in a sedan chair, but they can get a five star Mercat Tour guide!

CLOSES

The Royal Mile is perched on a long ridge of rock, with steep slopes to the north and south. Down these slopes plunge many wynds and closes. Closes are narrow streets between tenement buildings, once 'enclosed', shut off at night by a locked gate at either or both ends. Those to the north ended at the Nor' Loch, where Princes Street Gardens lie today. Those to the south ended at the Cowgate and Grassmarket. Have you ventured into any of the narrow, steep closes? Imagine making your way down to the bottom of the valley on foot in winter. Difficult. Try to get a cart down. Very difficult. Try to get a horse and carriage down. Impossible.

Advocate's Close, a typical Edinburgh close in the 19th century.

Public proclamations are made from the balcony of the Mercat Cross. Visitors also come here to find a guide.

Edinburgh, the 17th century Manhattan

Safety was very important to the people of Edinburgh, safety from English invasion.

For centuries we were hemmed in by city walls to the east, south and west and the Nor' Loch to the north. With a rapidly growing population, there was only one way to go, upwards. Edinburgh folk, not Americans, invented skyscrapers!

Tenement buildings in the closes today are up to seven storeys high, but they once reached ten, even fourteen storeys. The poor lived in cellars at the very bottom and attics at the very top while the wealthy lived in the middle.

Only in Edinburgh in the 1700s might a countess live in the same tenement as a fishmonger. Families at the top had a room with a view and were able to shake hands with the neighbour opposite. However, living conditions were grim. There were no pipes to take the dirty water out of people's homes. Instead we had 'the bucket'. It sat in the corner of one-roomed houses of poor families and filled up during the day with what we politely called 'nastiness'.

A map of Edinburgh as it was in 1647. Look at the tightly packed closes.

HORROR *of* HORRORS

By evening the bucket was overflowing with a thick yellow liquid and what looked like brown sausages floating on top. The smell was horrendous. But the town laws were strict. The 'Nastiness Act' told us we had to wait till after dark to get rid of the 'nasties'.

Imagine the scene at, say, 9.55pm, the housewives above, their sleeves rolled up, waiting for the curfew bell to strike ten. Shouting the warning 'Gardyloo!' (from the French 'prenez garde à l'eau', 'mind the water!') they emptied the 'nasties' down into the street below, along with all their other rubbish. If the dog or cat died that day it came hurtling down from above, gathering speed like a missile, splattering the walls. Yes, it rained cats and dogs. The 'nasties' piled up in the streets and attracted rats.

There was nothing romantic or picturesque about the Old Town. It was an overcrowded, filthy, disease-ridden slum. The most regular visitors were cholera, typhus, dysentery, invaders which walls and loch did not keep out.

Did you know?

The 'Nastiness Act' still exists. If you are strolling down a close after dark and you hear a cry of 'gardyloo' from above, do shout 'haud yer haun' (hold your hand / wait a minute).

You have ten seconds, not a minute, to duck. Now you know why locals carry umbrellas!

Daily life in an Old Town tenement.

Expansion Outwards

The 1700s brought great change to Scotland and therefore to Edinburgh.

In 1707 Scotland and England got married. The union of parliaments created one country, Great Britain. The English were no longer a threat but the Jacobite supporters of the exiled Stuarts were, till their defeat at Culloden in 1746. The city no longer needed walls, gates and a loch to keep out enemies.

The late 1700s was the time of the Scottish Enlightenment, an age of learning which gave Edinburgh the grand title, 'Athens of the North'. Dreadful living conditions in the Old Town were therefore more than an embarrassment.

Wealthy people saw a chance to make their dreams come true: they wanted to get away from the poor, they wanted fresh air, grand houses to show off their wealth, gardens, space for sedan chairs, carriages and horses. They wanted a city to be proud of.

In the 1750s plans were drawn up to expand the city to the north and south. Architect James Craig won a competition to design the New Town to the north. Architect Robert Adam drew up plans for expansion to the south with an area of fine houses at George Square and new university buildings.

BRIDGING THE GAP

The big problem was access to these areas. The steep narrow alleyways and closes were not suitable for wheeled carts, horses and carriages. The solution to the problem of access was to build two massive bridges to span the valleys on each side of the ridge.

The **NORTH BRIDGE**, begun in 1763, linked the High Street with the New Town. In 1769 a heavy rainstorm washed away some of the foundations. It collapsed, killing five workmen. When it was rebuilt, its open sides and iron railings caused both embarrassment and entertainment. Strong gusts of wind across the valley caused ladies skirts to fly up and blew passengers from the pavement into the mud in the middle of the bridge. The sides were later closed off.

Crossing the windswept North Bridge was a challenge, especially for Edinburgh ladies.

An artist's impression of the cross section of South Bridge, showing the vaulted chambers beneath.

The **SOUTH BRIDGE**, built 1785-88, linked the High Street with the University area. To this day it looks just like a road lined with tenements and shops. Those crossing it for the first time have no idea they are walking over a bridge until they reach a short stretch of railings half way across. This allows a view over the edge into the Cowgate in the valley below.

The completed bridge stretches **300 metres (1,000ft),** from the High Street, across the valley to the south to Nicholson Street. It is **18 metres (55ft) wide,** including pavements. It is supported by **22 arches, 19 of them** across the valley. The largest arch of the viaduct stands **9.3 metres (31ft) high, 9 metres (30ft) wide** and has foundations as far down as **6.6 metres (22ft)** into the bed rock.

Impressed? You should be!

The Cowgate arch of the South Bridge spans the bottom of the valley. This scene dates from 1818.

TO Build or NOT to Build

The task of building the bridge was a great challenge for the city. Lord Provost, Sir James Hunter Blair, was the man instrumental in building the bridge, though he died in 1787 before it was completed. Hunter Square and Blair Street, running down the valley, are named after him. Blair was part of a Board of Trustees which organised the project for the town council.

Opposition to the Bridge was fierce. The town council had to answer many questions posed by critics of the project.

Q Where will the money come from for such an expensive project?

A The bridge can be built without cost to the public purse. We'll buy property along the line of the bridge by compulsory purchase at its existing value. We'll then sell the land alongside the bridge for the building of modern tenements and shops at a profit. A large profit!

Q Who will build it?

A Robert Adam has submitted a grand expensive design. We'll choose a cheaper, less ambitious design by architect Robert Kay. Robert Adam will complain to the council but we must keep costs down.

Q Will wealthy residents in the Southside suburbs be included in an Edinburgh land or property tax?

A Areas of the South Side will benefit greatly from the new link with the High Street. They will therefore be included within the city boundaries and taxed.

Q How will our homes, businesses and streets be affected?

A We shall build new Edinburgh over the old. On the north side we'll demolish part of the Tron Kirk and three old streets, Peebles, Niddry's and Marlin's Wynds, and several streets on the south side. Owners of houses and businesses will be compensated. Stone from their properties can be recycled in the bridge itself.

Q Will the bridge be safe to cross? Look what happened to the North Bridge!

A We have every faith that contractor Alexander Laing will build a bridge which will be in use over two hundred years from now.

Q Will the exclusive Southside suburbs go downhill?

A Of course not, but residents can choose to move to the New Town.

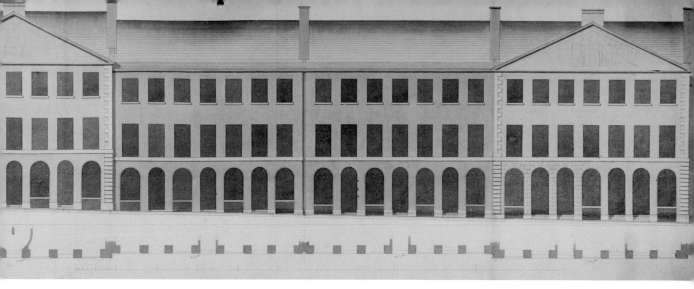

An elevation of the buildings along the South Bridge, probably prepared by Robert Kay in 1786. A standard house design was replicated along the Bridge.

POLITICAL STRING-PULLING

An important resident of Adam Square (now Chambers Street), Robert Dundas, Lord President of the Court of Session, objected to the gradient of the bridge. It would place his front door a few feet below street level. Passers-by might be able to peer in through his windows! The town council dared not oppose such an important judge, whose half-brother Henry Dundas, Viscount Melville, was on the Board of Trustees.

The final bridge sloped downward from the Tron Church, then rose sharply. The gradient was a thorn in the flesh of generations of Edinburgh horses and coach drivers. An ungrateful Dundas died before the bridge was fully opened! Wealthy families fled from the Adam Square area as it became commercialised.

LAYING THE FOUNDATION STONE

On 1st August 1785 the foundation stone was laid with great solemnity, say the chroniclers of the day, by the Grand Master Mason of Scotland, Lord Haddo, in the presence of the great and the good, Lord Provost and Magistrates, nobility and gentry. Thousands of locals turned out to watch the grand procession make its way from the High Street to the foot of Niddry's Wynd. The stone of the archway over the Cowgate was laid. A 'time capsule' containing coins of the time and a grand Latin inscription, was laid with the foundation stone.

The bridge took three years to build but was opened to foot traffic in November 1776. Poet Robert Burns had just arrived in Edinburgh for the first time. He may have been among the first to use the footbridge! Lord Cockburn in his 'Memorials' recalled being dragged, as a boy in 1787, to the High School to enrol as a pupil. His only enjoyment was the challenge of crossing builders' planks over the arches.

Is the Bridge Cursed?

The grand opening ceremony took place in 1788. A rich elderly widow from Adam Square had watched the building work with interest. She wanted to be the first to cross.

She had friends in high places and her wish was granted, though she had to cross in a coffin as she died days before the opening.

Superstitious locals watched the six black horses with plumed feathers pull the hearse carrying her casket across the bridge. Remembering the collapse of the North Bridge almost twenty years before, they looked on this as a bad omen and even refused to cross it.

An artist's impression of the corpse crossing the bridge at the grand opening ceremony in 1788.

The South Bridge in the 1830s where wealthy people went to shop and be seen.

EDINBURGH'S FIRST PURPOSE BUILT SHOPPING CENTRE

Land on the site of the proposed bridge was bought up as cheaply as possible. Written sources estimate the cost of building the bridge was anything from £6,500 to £15,000. Land on the sides of the bridge was then sold in batches at a huge profit for up to £50 per foot. It was one of the most expensive pieces of real estate in Europe. 'Location, Location, Location' sang the estate agents of the time!

Businessmen lined the top of the bridge with fashionable shops. In February 1788 a writer in a journal of the day speaks of the shops on both sides of the Bridge as having been finished

> 'with a degree of elegance and convenience of which, till of late, we had no conception'.

Rents for shops were £35-£60 a year and for vaults, £20-£40. Entrances to vaults, and more shops, were located on Blair and Niddry Streets.

We know from the 1790 Street Directory that there were about 100 businesses operating from the South Bridge. Many were linked with cloth and clothing, such as glovers, hat makers and tailors. There were confectioners and grocers, goldsmiths and jewellers, upholsterers and cabinet makers. Printers, publishers and booksellers set up close to the university. There were at least ten wine merchants. Later, coffee houses and taverns were set up. Businessmen, teachers, surgeons and architects also lived on the Bridge.

South Bridge Street Directory, 1790

23	Mrs. Mathieson – vintner
24	James Burns – haberdasher
25	John Guthrie – bookseller
28	George Gregory – tin-plate worker
30	Thomas Morgan – watchmaker
31	John Eelbeck – seal engraver
37	McVicar & Blair – linen drapers
	William McLean – merchant
38	Alexander McGill – shoemaker

A Wee Problem

The cobblers, cutlers, smelters, grocers, milliners, drapers, wine merchants and jewellers who set up shop very soon shut up shop!

The workmen who built the bridge ignored the fact that here in Edinburgh, only occasionally mind you, it rains! Due to a tight budget, they did not waterproof the bridge properly with puddling clay.

The bridge began to leak, and not just rain water! Human sewage – 'nasties'– and droppings from horses crossing the bridge, oozed down through the vaults. Flooding was such a serious problem that, within 20 years, businesses began to move out. The first evidence was a jeweller who boarded up his workshop in 1796. Others followed suit up to the 1820s.

POPULATION, POPULATION, POPULATION

Great changes taking place in Edinburgh in the early 1800s affected the vaults. The population of the city grew rapidly. It also shifted. Professional classes, such as lawyers and doctors, moved from the Old Town to the spacious residential New Town. However, despite their departure and two cholera epidemics, the population in the Old Town grew by at least 50%. At a time of great changes in farming and industry, unemployed flocked from countryside to city to find work. Highlanders, forced off their lands in the Clearances, and Irish immigrants flooded in.

The Old Town could not cope. Houses once owned by the wealthy were subdivided again and again into smaller flats, many with only one room.

Edinburgh really was a Jekyll and Hyde city! Robert Louis Stevenson observed in his *Edinburgh Picturesque Notes* in the 1860s:

> 'Social inequality is nowhere more ostentatious than at Edinburgh . . . to look over the South Bridge and see the Cowgate below full of crying hawkers, is to view one rank of society from another in the twinkling of an eye.'

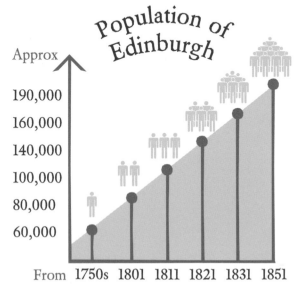

Population of Edinburgh

Approx

190,000
160,000
140,000
100,000
80,000
60,000

From 1750s 1801 1811 1821 1831 1851

The graph shows the rapid growth of the population of Edinburgh.

FROM BAD TO WORSE

As Edinburgh changed, so did the vaults. They provided 'unofficial' shelter for the poorest of the poor, spilling over from nearby streets like Blackfriar's Wynd and the Cowgate, known as 'Little Ireland'. People who squatted in the vaults had nowhere else to go. They used the vaults as a place of refuge.

Squatters left material evidence of their stay in midden or rubbish heaps. There is little written evidence of their presence, as most were squatting illegally. Brothel owners, prostitutes and criminals also moved into what became Edinburgh's latest red light district.

ABANDONMENT

Conditions became so bad that by the 1860s most vaults had been emptied. Chambers were filled in with rubble to avoid flooding. This also gave security to businesses still operating above, on street level, and discouraged squatters and criminals. Many of the original flagstones were removed from the floors before they were filled in as part of an attempt to salvage and recycle what was useful.

OUT OF SIGHT, OUT OF MIND

The vaults were largely forgotten till the 1980s. It is likely that during WWII some vaults were used as air raid shelters. Local residents remember that some vaults had to be pumped out as they were full of water. They were afraid of going down in to the darkness, some claiming that there were 'bad spirits' at work!

The overspill from overcrowded Blackfriar's Wynd may have found shelter in the vaults.

Rediscovery

The opening up of the vaults began in the 1980s when Norrie Rowan, a former international rugby player, became a property owner and builder in the Old Town.

During the 1980s he owned the Tron Bar on Hunter Square. He gradually bought or leased property on both sides of Blair Street and in Niddry Street.

While developing his property in Blair Street he discovered a section of a medieval street built in the 1530s linking the High Street and Cowgate. Marlin's Wynd is thought to have been the first formal paved street to be laid out in Edinburgh, named after Walter Merlyoun, a French mason. It was demolished in the 1780s to make way for the bridge.

Mr Rowan spent over ten years clearing out many of the vaults, using pick, spade, shovel and wheelbarrow. It was no mean feat, as many of the chambers were filled almost to the ceiling with earth and rubble. Some rooms had stalactites up to two metres long.

Stalactites hang from vaulted ceilings due to the water seeping down.

In the early 1990s Mr Rowan contacted Des Brogan, Director of Mercat Tours. The decision was made to open the vaults to visitors, giving them the opportunity to discover the history which lay beneath the bridge. Some rooms, which Mercat uses today, were not originally open to the public as they were still inaccessible. Today, there are few vaults which have not been reopened. Although the vaults have been made structurally safe and sympathetic lighting has been installed, visitors view them largely as they were two hundred years ago.

Vaults were filled with tonnes of rubble.

A STEAMY ENCOUNTER!

Workmen, excavating in the semi-darkness in 1994, heard unearthly groans coming from the wall where they were working. The hairs on the back of their necks stood on end as the groans got louder, but they pulled themselves together and continued hammering away. Suddenly the wall collapsed. As they peered through the opening, they heard an almighty scream. Enough was enough. They took to their heels as if the Devil himself was after them. Their boss came down to investigate. He discovered they had knocked through to a room in the sauna on Blair Street!

Blair Street Vaults today look very similar to what they were like 200 years ago.

Descend and Discover

The entrance to the vaults is half way down Blair Street at Number 28. Our room by room tour begins here.

The Mercat Tours office, Interpretation Room and shop are at ground level. Two flights of stairs take us to the lowest level of the vaults, where the ground is rough and uneven. All tours follow a circular route as can be seen from the plan.

{ Access to Rooms 1 and 2 is from a corridor under a block of tenement buildings on Blair Street. }

1 KETTLE ROOM

The chamber has a delivery chute high up in the wall, brick shelves and a stone fireplace. At first a storage room, the fireplace would later have made it attractive to squatters. The large iron kettle, on display in our interpretation room above, was found in this room.

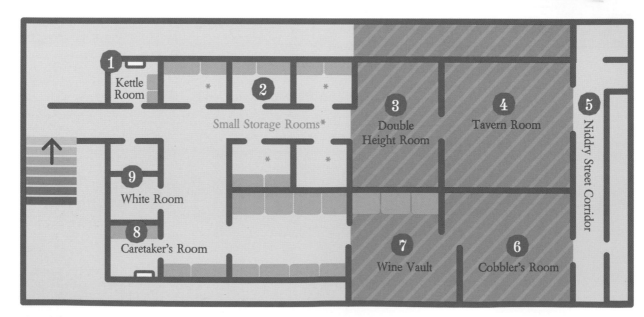

Plan of Blair Street Vaults. The shaded rooms are actually under the Bridge.

2 STORAGE ROOMS

Several small rooms along the corridor have brick shelves which housed goods and valuables. Reference numbers for storage space are painted on some walls. Many chambers once had thick, heavy doors with wooden or iron locks to keep goods stored inside secure. We can see where the doors were fastened to the walls. Locks and pieces of wooden doors have survived but most of the wood has rotted away and the valuables are long gone.

Privately owned vaults had heavy wooden doors and locks to secure valuables stored inside.

3 DOUBLE HEIGHT ROOM

{ We are now under the bridge itself. }

The arch above is divided into three floors. The ceiling of the bottom floor fell or was knocked down to fill up the room after the vaults were abandoned. There is a gap in the ceiling of the floor above, which leads into the third and top room. Above that is an arch of the South Bridge. The traffic rumbling across the bridge above us cannot be heard at this level. We may, however, both hear and feel the water dripping down!

Rooms of this size were likely to be used at first as workshops for craftsmen, assisted by their wives and children. Street directories from the time list merchants living above the vaults, without detail of their trade. However, they also list small scale craftsmen working in leather and metal, such as boot and shoemakers, engravers, tin-plate workers, watch makers and cutlers. Some are likely to have used the vaults, using entrances from Blair and Niddry Streets.

The 'double height' room was created when the ceiling of the lower vault fell down or was knocked down.

4 TAVERN ROOM

Piles of oyster shells were found when this room was cleared out. Cheap and nutritious, oysters were once part of the staple diet of the poor. In the 1700s it was common for different classes of society to mingle in dark cellars below taverns to drink claret and beer and dine on oysters. There is evidence of taverns operating from the South Bridge. It is possible that this room was at one stage an oyster cellar or drinking den.

{ What would an oyster cellar look like on a Saturday night over 200 years ago? }

Perhaps you can hear

- The fiddler striking up a tune
- The drunks singing along, stamping their feet on the straw
- The coarse laughter, bawdy jokes
- The variety of accents, soft spoken Highlanders, Irish brogue, Lowland Scots, King's English

Perhaps you can smell

- Damp
- Body odours
- Cigar and pipe tobacco smoke
- Fish

A Tour of the Vaults

Artist's impression of an oyster bar 200 years ago.

WALLS CAN BE FASCINATING!

Random rubble walls with stones of varying shapes and sizes can be seen in the vaults. Bones have been found in the mortar. We do not know which animals they belonged to, but they are probably a waste product. Imagine a builder chewing on a meaty bone during his break then throwing it into the mortar!

Oyster shell fragments have also been found in mortar in the walls of the vaults. Why oyster shells? In the 1700s 'scaffengers' collected washed shells from oyster bars, along with rubbish from the streets. They sold shells to builders, who put them into walls for extra strength as a binding agent for mortar. It is therefore possible that some of the oyster shells found in the vaults were intended for building purposes.

Did you know?

Superstitious folk believed shells in their homes would ward off evil spirits.

Digging out of this area revealed the tiny workshop of a jeweller, James Henderson. Watch faces and gold rings were found.

The door to his workshop, with his name on it, is on the landing half way up the stairs. The skeleton is not that of the jeweller!

5 NIDDRY STREET CORRIDOR

The most popular use of privately owned vaults today is pubs and clubs, just as it was 200 years ago! The clubs have changed somewhat from the early 1800s, when gentlemen's clubs were popular in the city: the Dirty Club, Dirty Linen Club, Long Beard Club, Wig Club to name but a few.

The most notorious of all was the Hell-Fire Club. Local worthy Robert Chambers in his *Traditions of Edinburgh*, describes a

> '…terrible and infamous association of wild young men … met in various profound places throughout Edinburgh … I have conversed with old people who had seen the last worn-out members of the Hell-Fire Club … believed to have been an association in compact with the Prince of Darkness … their president was named the Devil.'

Perhaps one of the 'profound' meeting places was in the vaults? Imagine carriages rolling up at an entrance and respected pillars of Edinburgh society, wearing black hoods, disappearing into the vaults. Their pleasures were drugs – opium or cocaine – and prostitutes. We believe there were several brothels in the vaults but the exact sites are unknown.

{ We turn to the right to retrace our steps under the bridge, into room 6. }

COBBLER'S ROOM

When the debris was cleared out, many pieces of leather, old shoes and small nails were found. We believe the room may have been the workshop of a leather worker or cobbler. Leather scraps may also be linked with bookbinders, but they tended to set up shop on the other side of the valley nearer to the University area.

The remains of stalactites on the ceiling are a reminder of the dampness of the vaults, the reason why legal businesses abandoned them in the early 1800s.

A Tour of the Vaults

How a leather workers' workshop might have looked 200 years ago.

{ What would such a workshop be like 200 years ago? }

Perhaps you can hear

- Hammering
- Dripping water
- Constant coughing of workers whose lungs are ruined

Perhaps you can smell

- Fish oil burning in the cruisie lamps on the walls
- The tallow candles, made of mutton fat
- Ammonia from the urine of the workers and from horses crossing the bridge above
- Body odour from workers who rarely wash themselves or their clothes

This piece of a leather boot was found in the vaults

This vault may have been a workshop for leather workers.

Fresh Corpses for Sale

The vaults became home to criminals, the most infamous of whom were the bodysnatchers.

In Scotland several hundred years ago, there were very strict laws about how many corpses could be dissected in medical students' anatomy classes. Before the Anatomy Act of 1832 only corpses of executed criminals were to be used as it was believed that a 'dissected person' could not go to heaven. Demand for corpses far outstripped supply.

An enterprising group of Edinburgh criminals, the bodysnatchers, were happy to supply corpses. Their aim was not to assist medical knowledge. They could earn up to £10 for a corpse in good condition; as much money as some might earn in a whole year in more honest employment. The drawbacks were the long hours of work, gruesome nature of the job and the risk of being caught and punished.

Did you know?

The theft of the shroud, rather than the corpse carried the death penalty! A careful bodysnatcher would be sure to leave the grave clothes behind.

The crypt you can see here would have had an iron gate across the entrance originally.

Edinburgh folk dreaded and feared the bodysnatchers. The rich placed mortsafes of iron bars over the grave to protect the body, or employed watchmen in lookout towers. The poor could only pray that their loved ones would rest in peace.

The bodysnatchers worked by day as well as by night. By day they visited Edinburgh graveyards to watch funerals taking place. When they returned in the middle of the night, they knew the location of fresh corpses and where to dig. It was a winter job. The corpses did not decompose as readily in the cold and the dark nights provided excellent cover. However, as the demand for corpses grew, they risked using the few hours of darkness in summer time. This increased their need of storage facilities for the corpses en route to the dissection table.

The bodysnatchers needed somewhere to hide the bodies

- with a fairly cool constant temperature

- near the Canongate and Greyfriars graveyards

- near the medical schools in the area

We believe that the vaults, ideal for storing wine and beer, were also used as a half-way house to store corpses.

Artist's impression of the bodysnatchers using the vaults for storage of corpses.

Late 1700s 'black glass' claret bottles.

⑦ WINE VAULT

Think Scotland, think whisky or Irn Bru. Think Edinburgh, think beer brewing. However, in the 1700s, Lowland Scotland's national drink was claret. French ships carrying the Bordeaux wine docked at the port of Leith, two miles to the north. Edinburgh wine merchants would carry out a most reliable form of market research. They boarded the ships, bought a few barrels, set them on carts with a roast pig and drove them through the streets. Edinburgh folk, armed with mugs and jars, paid a small amount of money for a sample. If they gave the thumbs up, the merchants returned to Leith to stock up and bottle the wine.

There were many vintners in this area. They were delighted to have such excellent storage facilities in the vaults, in the heart of the Old Town. The now empty bins were stacked with claret bottles, laid out on sawdust, with a cushion of straw between the layers. They were left to mature at an ideal temperature. The numbers painted on the shelves refer to stock lots. When the room was cleared out, sawdust, straw, wine glasses and claret bottles were found. Beer was also stored in the vaults, which explains the finding of barrel hoops.

Storage of wine and beer was one of the original and legal uses of the vaults. However when criminals moved in, things became interesting!

Storage bins once housed large quantities of claret.

STILL WATERS RUN DEEP

During the Napoleonic Wars of the early 1800s, when Britain was at war with France, French goods were not allowed into Scotland. Lowland drinkers, deprived of wine and brandy, turned to another tipple, whisky, brought south by Highlanders migrating to the city. Getting a licence to distil it was difficult so hundreds of illegal stills sprang up. With Napoleon's defeat in 1815, customs officers turned their attention to finding these stills.

When excise officers, following a tip off, raided the vaults, they found a still which had been operating for at least 18 months 'at great injury to the revenue'. They seized large quantities of wines, casks, mash tubs and other equipment.

The gang had shown daring and ingenuity. They had covered their tracks by bricking up and plastering over the original door and using a hidden entry. We do not know the exact location of the still in the vaults. We do know that the gang drew water from a supply pipe to homes on the bridge which belonged to a local water company. Cheeky! They fitted a soil pipe so that smoke escaping upwards would not be noticed on the bridge. An old maid, muttering madly, carried out the flagons of the rough 'firewater', hidden in a green bag under her cloak. It was sold to Edinburgh dealers who asked no awkward questions.

In the 1820s it became cheaper to obtain a licence for the distillation of whisky. Illegal production therefore declined.

The illicit still in the vaults was just one of many in the area.

8 THE CARETAKER'S ROOM

{ We now return to the area under the block of tenement building of 28 Blair Street. }

The vault was used at one stage for storing wine. A dividing wall between the bins has been removed to lengthen one shelf. It may have been used as a bed by a caretaker guarding the valuable stock.

After the legal businesses moved out in the 1820s the room is likely to have attracted squatters because of the fireplace. The chimney runs up the height of the tenement, straight at first, then at an angle to create an up draught to draw smoke upwards and prevent rain from falling onto the fire.

{ What would living conditions have been like for squatters? }

Perhaps you can hear

- The screaming of a hungry baby
- The moaning of a sick child
- The crying of a young mother in despair

Perhaps you can smell

- Animal bones simmering in a pot over the fire
- The bucket of 'nasties' in the corner

Artist's impression of a vault as a refuge for squatters.

⑨ WHITE ROOM

On the left of the door frame is a rounded smooth, carved stone from the 12th century. There is evidence to suggest that it was recycled from the ruined Holyrood Abbey. Stone from the older streets, which were demolished, was also used in the building of the vaults.

We are not sure what this small white-washed vault was used for. On the back wall is a small bricked up 'window'. It was possibly a shaft to borrow light from the area above or a delivery chute for delivering goods into the vaults, or both. Coal, for example, could be dropped down the chute, instead of being carried down the spiral staircase. Scraps of leather were also found. Perhaps it was a leather worker's storeroom or workshop, later occupied by squatters. We can only imagine how such conditions might have affected the health of those living or working in a room like this.

12th century carved stone.

On the back wall of the white-washed vault is a bricked up light shaft or delivery chute.

Life in Edinburgh – 'Nasty, Brutish and Short'

In the early 1700s in Scotland, a man's life expectancy was 27 years.

By the late 1700s it was 39 years, younger for those using the vaults. Workers were prone to arthritis, rheumatism, tuberculosis and lung conditions.

Ill-health was also caused by dreadful living conditions. Documentary evidence from the 1850s and 60s reveals how bad conditions were in slum tenements of Blackfriar's Wynd and the Cowgate, close to the South Bridge. Social reformers showed that such conditions were responsible for the high death rate and widespread ill-health in the form of cholera, dysentery, tuberculosis, scarlet fever and typhus.

> In the 1860s, a Slum Clearance Act, combined with the efforts of Edinburgh's first Medical Officer of Health, led to the demolition of slum housing and a gradual improvement in living conditions and health in the Old Town.

What was happening above ground was reflected in change underground. By the 1860s many of the vaults in this section were already abandoned. Rubble from tenements in nearby streets, which were demolished, may also have been piled up in the vaults. Remaining criminals and squatters would be forced to move out.

The vaults were no longer a place of refuge for the poorest of the poor. However they more recently became a place of refuge for a Romanian asylum seeker!

ESCAPE!

In 1989 a Romanian Rugby team came to Edinburgh to play the locals at Murrayfield. The team was escorted by six officials in dark suits, President Ceausescu's secret police. At the invitation of Norrie Rowan, they had a farewell drink with the Scottish team at the Tron Bar in Hunter Square. One, Christian Raducanu, talked about his wish to defect. The barman took Christian down to the cellar, helped him to tear a grille off the wall, stand on a barrel and squeeze through a ventilation shaft into the vaults.

For hours the 'minders' searched for him without success. The team flew home without him. From the vaults he made his way into the street, stopped a police car and asked for political asylum. He was granted a British passport, and became a P.E. teacher. In December 1989 Ceausescu's communist regime was ended.

Did you know?

In the late 1800s a doctor visited a patient on the 8th floor of a tenement near to the South Bridge. On arrival, he came face to face with an enormous pig. How had it got up so many stairs? The patient explained the pig had been born there and had never been downstairs! The doctor was Sir Arthur Conan Doyle.

MEGGET'S CELLAR

{ Half way up the narrow spiral staircase is our cellar. }

It is called Megget's Cellar after a leather merchant called Aitken Megget. In the 1820s he had his business at Number 28 Blair Street, now the site of our Mercat Tours office. In this room, visitors on some of our tours have a seat, a drink and hear some stories about the vaults.

Megget's Cellar provides an atmospheric location for story telling.

The Story of Mary McKinnon

In the early 1820s a tavern on the South Bridge, close to Blair Street Vaults, was owned and run by a Mary McKinnon. Although outwardly respectable, it was actually a house of ill-repute. Mary was its mistress, keeping a close eye on her girls and their customers. Business boomed. Mary grew wealthy. She gained a reputation for a hot temper and strong will.

One evening in February 1823, disaster struck. While Mary was absent, a group of drunken men staggered in. The women were violently attacked and furniture was broken: the tavern was in uproar. On her return, Mary was knocked to the floor. It appears that she grabbed a table knife and swung it at William Mowatt, a young clerk. The blade pierced his left side and he was mortally wounded. He died twelve days later in the local Infirmary, having identified Mary as his attacker.

Mary pleaded not guilty at her trial but the all-male jury quickly returned a guilty verdict. On April 16th 1823 Mary was 'hanged by the neck until dead' in front of a crowd of 20,000 people. Her corpse was dissected in public by Dr Alexander Munro, Professor of Anatomy at Edinburgh University. Her skeleton may yet be hanging in a medical school today, her organs preserved in vinegar.

INTERPRETATION ROOM

Most tours end in the interpretation room, giving visitors the opportunity to view information boards and artefacts, pick up the kettle and drop it on their big toe, smell the fish oil . . .

Crucibles were used for smelting metal.

Snuff box

Among the artefacts found in the vaults were a grinding wheel and twelve cracked and worn clay pots, crucibles for smelting metal. Such equipment could have been used by a cutler. Cutlers made knives and forks, scissors and surgical instruments. Minute particles from the grinding stone and the blades, coupled with poor ventilation, would ruin their lungs.

They were both quite eccentric. They had a mill for grinding snuff in Colinton and came into Edinburgh in a bright yellow coach, to catch up with all the gossip. At the site of their snuff shop on the High Street, carved today on the wall, is an image of James Gillespie.

This grinding wheel may have been used by a cutler. There were several on South Bridge.

A plaque which marks the site of his shop at 231 High Street shows Gillespie's bulbous nose and protruding pointed chin.

One of the many artefacts on display is a little snuff box. Snuff was very popular in 18th century Edinburgh. The rich would put it on the back of their hands and sniff it up so as not to smell all the nastiness on the streets. A famous snuff merchant in Edinburgh was James Gillespie who was in partnership with his brother.

Did you know?

Snuff was sometimes laced with cocaine, which was perfectly legal in those days.

SEDAN CHAIR

This was the taxi of the 1700s as closes and wynds were too narrow for horses and carriages. Chairmen at both front and back had to be strong – they were often burly Highlanders. There was a deluxe version with tilted seat so a person would not fall out. One judge hired a chair if it was raining to take his wig home. He walked!

In the 1740s a sedan chair was even used by bodysnatchers! One day a corpse was discovered in a side street near the bustling High Street, on its way to the Medical School and dissection room. The chairmen were banished from the city and the sedan chair burned by the common hangman. We do not know what happened to the corpse!

Cruisie lamps, which burned fish oil, were used to light the vaults.

Many horseshoes were found in the vaults.

Animal bones may be remains of a tasty dinner 200 years ago!

A replica sedan chair, which was a popular form of transport in the narrow streets of the Old Town.

A novelty pistol shaped glass bottle.

{ Our historic vaults tour is ended. Are any of you brave enough to go on a ghost tour? }

Hidden & Haunted

'Possibly the most haunted place in Britain.'
BBC

Mercat Tours first used Blair Street Vaults in 1996 to tell ghost stories of old Edinburgh above in an atmospheric location.

From the earliest days of the tours, the spirits of the vaults made us aware of their presence. A pattern emerged.

- people saw figures when the rest of the vaults were empty

- heard footsteps when everyone was standing still

- felt changes in temperature when there was no source of a draught

- experienced changes in atmosphere from one vault to another

- captured orbs, circles of bright light, white, blue or even black on camera

One psychic said of her visit in May 1996:

'From the moment I looked around the grim setting, I felt that we were not alone. Oh, we had about a dozen other tourists with us, but it was more than that. The room held a lingering sense of immense sorrow and hardship.

The sensations in the rooms became more sinister as the tour continued. I could see the outline of figures, and the rooms threatened to transform into something dark and tragic.'

The atmospheric passageways are home to many strange, ghostly experiences.

A Ghost tour enters the wine vault.

Some spirits in the vaults are interactive spirits

- ghosts of deceased persons who are grounded in the environment, trapped here by tragedy or 'unfinished business'

- they make themselves known in many ways, cause mischief and grab our attention

- very few have evil intent but there are exceptions

- there have been rare occurrences of a form of physical or vocal possession.

Some spirits are residual

- they retrace steps taken in life, like a video or DVD playing back a scene

- they do not notice our presence and are no threat.

Our written records include hundreds of accounts of paranormal activity experienced by people on our tours, guides and psychics. We shall share with you details of some of the most frequently seen or experienced interactive spirits.

'The Most Systematic Investigation of a Haunted Location in the World'

an entry in the Guinness Book of World Records, 2002

By 2001 the Vaults had gained such an international reputation for being haunted that they became the focus for a scientific study, the Edinburgh Ghost Project.

The investigation was led by Professor Richard Wiseman of the University of Hertfordshire, a psychologist with a particular interest in the paranormal.

A thermal imager, thermometers and air movement detectors were used in one part of the experiment. 218 volunteers also took part. They were brought down to the vaults in small groups of about ten at a time, over a period of four days. They spent ten minutes alone in randomly allocated rooms and recorded their impressions of the space and any paranormal type of activity. 44% of the volunteers reported paranormal activity ranging from an unusual change in temperature, strange smells and sounds, burning sensations and a strong sense of being watched, to a detailed description of a well-known apparition.

Before the experiment, Mercat used past experience to grade the rooms in an order from 'most' to 'least' haunted. The grades were kept secret, under lock and key and only known to one person. After the Ghost Project, the public data was compared to Mercat's secret grading. The three rooms assessed as most active by Mercat were the three most active rooms during the experiment. 51% of experiences were in these rooms. Read on to find out which ones they were!

3 DOUBLE HEIGHT ROOM

It is the largest in the vaults, one room on top of another. It is also the THIRD most active room. Dogs find this room particularly disturbing. They bark, whimper, or refuse to enter. Common experiences include dramatic changes in temperature and a menacing atmosphere. A bird-like apparition has been known to swoop down, clawing at people in the group. A naked man has been seen floating in what would have been the next floor up, close to the doorway. Our advice is, if you don't want a shock, don't look up!

Follow me if you dare!

The Aristocrat

A ghost, witnessed more and more frequently since the first sighting in 2005, is that of a well to-do aristocrat. A tall man with a tall black hat and a beard, he stands to the right of the entrance between the double height room and the tavern room. Psychics have suggested a possible name Finnion or Gerain McKenzie. He leans against the wall, arms folded, watching and grinning at people as they pass. At present he seems to view those in the vaults with curiosity rather than hostility. Could he have been a member of the Hell-Fire Club?

4 TAVERN ROOM

For many years this room was paranormally 'quiet', though it is situated between two highly active spaces. In more recent years there have been experiences of sighs and screaming, a black mass moving along the ceiling and a dark figure moving through the room. Some have described feelings of drunkenness, an inability to walk and extreme giggling. We do think it was once a drinking den!

The 'aristocrat' may be curious about our style of dress.

The Tavern room has become a more 'active' area in recent years.

⑤ NIDDRY STREET CORRIDOR

Niddry Street Corridor has been the scene of sightings and experiences since the earliest days of our tours. It was here that our growing number of experiences took a sinister turn.

A guide described the experience of a visitor on her tour:

> 'She told us to wait behind her. She stood there for a minute looking ahead of her. Then she suddenly stumbled backwards. Later she told us of the presence of a malevolent male ghost who was very strong … He had told her to get out of the vaults, and she had tried to reason with him, saying she respected that this was his territory … He then made a lunge at her, and she saw him very clearly. She described him as a big man, wearing a filthy blue overcoat and carrying something jagged in his hand – a knife perhaps, or a broken bottle. He said 'Get out!' repeatedly. He was very territorial.'

You will find out more about this malevolent interactive spirit shortly.

Niddry Street Corridor is a very interactive area with regard to Electro Magnetic Field (EMF) and digital camera records.

⑥ COBBLER'S ROOM

{ This is the second most 'active' room. }

The room takes its name from a 'happy' spirit, believed to be that of a shoemaker from the late 1700s to early 1800s. First detected and described in 1997, he is usually seen in the south-west corner. Bald, short and stocky, in his early 50s, he wears a long leather apron over a white shirt. He is busy working at a bench or stool. He seems to enjoy our company as he is often laughing or smiling. He shows great interest in our footwear and has been known to tug at shoelaces. He seems puzzled by Velcro! Psychics have advised us to go to this room if we have difficulties in the vaults. The strong, positive, benign spirit of the cobbler will protect us.

However the room is not friendly to everyone. Activity in this area includes the physical movement of objects, the most common being the throwing of stones. They tend to be heard hitting the walls. Some have actually seen them whizzing across the room.

Veiled Woman

Female visitors standing near the north-west corner, sometimes experience tears, grief, anger, even physical pain across the abdomen. Some feel they are being pushed away from the corner. Such darker feelings are linked to a youngish woman, dressed in black. She is veiled, either physically or psychologically as she tries to hide her grief. Psychics have described her as very disturbed, possibly due to a deeply traumatic experience connected with childbirth. Did a tragedy involving a child cause her death, either through suicide or a broken heart? We do try to let her grieve in peace.

The 'Happy Spirit', the cobbler, likes to study our footwear, in particular, trainers!

⑦ WINE VAULT

Some apparitions are fixed in one room – more or less to the spot – and do not venture far out of their corners. Others have the ability to move and walk around.

Jack's hidey hole.

Play with me!

The Mischief Maker

A spirit who wanders freely through the vaults, but is most often to be found in the Wine Vault, is a wee boy, Jack or James. He is thought to be about six to eight years old, with blond curly hair. He is dressed in a smart blue suit with knicker-bocker trousers and white frilly shirt. He happily sits in a lower shelf, watching the passersby but also moves around and through groups.

He is mostly drawn to children, guide dogs or women. He holds the hands of women in a cold but not unpleasant way. Does he see them as a mother figure?

He is sometimes playing with a red ball. He can be heard singing and chuckling.

A child described her encounter with Jack:

> 'I felt a strange cold hand grip my hand … I though it was my mum but she had gloves on. It was very weird because I heard a little voice laughing playfully … I think he wanted to play with me … Strange!'

However Jack may also shows signs of fear. Visitors experience his feelings and sometimes a sharp tugging on the hems and sleeves of their clothes. He seems to try to stop them entering the Blair Street corridor ahead. Why would he do that?

8 CARETAKER'S ROOM

A man is seen in the room which bears his name, sitting by the fireplace, his legs outstretched, a glass in his hand. Mineral water? Unlikely! More commonly seen is his companion, a small wiry-haired terrier-like dog. Some only catch sight of its wagging tail. It sniffs about and brushes against visitors' legs. Fortunately it does not mistake a leg for a lamppost!

In the late 1990s a group of 12-year-old girls on a birthday celebration tour were listening to a tale in this room. A little girl standing in front of the fireplace started to fidget and rub the side of her leg. The guide asked if she was alright and got the reply 'I'm fine, it's just that the fire is too hot'. There was a stunned silence. Everyone looked behind her. There had probably not been a fire lit there for over 150 years!

The wine bin corridor leads to the caretaker's room.

Guarding the wine and sampling it!

⑨ The White Room – The Most Active Room

We have had more strange and extreme occurrences in this room than any other and this was confirmed by the Ghost Project.

Many sense a 'bad feeling', a 'wall' which prevents them from entering. Is this the room Jack does not want us to enter?

On one tour when a man with an Electromagnetic Field recorder did enter, he watched the gauge go off the scale, such was the activity and energy of the spirit inside (an EMF detects electrical charges in the environment).

It is in this room that our most unpleasant spirit seems to manifest most often. We call him Mr Boots, as he wears knee-length leather boots and his footsteps are heard echoing throughout the vaults. He is also known as 'the watcher'. He stalks groups round the vaulted chambers with one exception. He has not been experienced in the 'safe' Cobbler's room. You have already read about a confrontation with him in Niddry Street corridor.

We hold him responsible for various disturbances which take place from time to time.

- electric lights flicker and go out

- candles turn blue and go out, though there are no draughts or people near them

- guides find their torches do not work

- during investigations recorders and dictaphones fail to work

- visitors have problems with their cameras

- batteries drain

- watches stop

A malevolent spirit stalks visitors in the vaults.

He particularly does not like us entering the White Room and, most disturbingly, has caused actual physical pain to those who have ventured into this room. Some have described an aching back pain, pressure on head and shoulders, or a choking sensation. After leaving the vaults, some victims have found scratch marks or bruises on the lower back and shoulder areas of their bodies.

An encounter with Mr Boots can be very disturbing:

> '... all throughout the tour I was fine ... until I entered the last room ... I got a strong smell of whisky which was followed by breathing on the back of my neck and side of neck as if somebody was trying to tell me something ... I felt as if something was choking me because I found it hard to breathe ... I asked the guide if this had happened before. Her reply was yes ... I had to leave the room'.

There are also occasions when Mr Boots leaves his mark on unsuspecting visitors:

> '... had his back to the opening and felt himself forcibly moved. When we reached our hotel, ... removed his sweater and found two deep red marks on his back where he had felt the hands on him'.

It has been suggested that Mr Boots was a bodysnatcher storing 'the goods' in the White Room, or a murderer. Both possibilities would explain the paranormal stench of death. It has also been suggested that he was a slum landlord, extorting money from his poor tenants with threats. Perhaps he was both. Recently he has been heard to shout, 'My name is Edward'. He does not like our nicknames for him!

In 2005 a photo was taken in this room whilst it was in complete darkness. It shows a face which matches the descriptions of our malevolent friend. The image we have has been adapted using contrast and brightness so it can be seen on paper. What do you think?

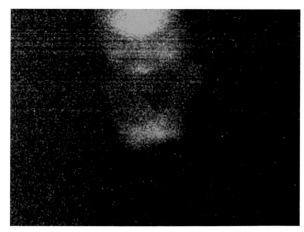

Face to face with Mr Boots? This was taken in the White Room.

{ Are the ghosts real or figments of overactive imagination powered by suggestion? You must decide that for yourselves as you visit the vaults in person. }

THE VAULTS TODAY

There has been no major reconstruction of the South Bridge to date, but many changes have taken place in vaulted areas beneath it. Some now house nightclubs, corporate hospitality venues and even a theatre. The area of Blair Street Vaults is one of the few parts of the South Bridge left in its original state, actually under street level. Electricity has been installed but the damp, dark, bare chambers still retain their original character and atmosphere. This enables us to sense the history and imagine what it was like to live and work in Edinburgh over two hundred years ago and perhaps experience the spirits of those who remain.

HISTORY IS A DAMN GOOD STORY. WHAT IT NEEDS IS DAMN GOOD TELLING.

This is the motto of the founder of Mercat Tours, Des Brogan. Every year our guides take countless groups through Blair Street Vaults. Whether a visitor is on an historical or ghost tour, as they head down the stairs into the darkness, who knows what they will experience, apart from a quality tour! We bring the vaults to life through storytelling, rather than props, gimmicks or special effects. We provide visitors with an entertaining, enthralling and historically accurate look at a unique feature of Edinburgh's hidden past. Hopefully this booklet has done just that too but you will agree that it is not quite the same as viewing them in person. So do come back and visit us again.

We are grateful to the following for permission to reproduce images:

Reproduced by permission of the Trustees of the National Library of Scotland inside cover & p 6; Patrick Geddes Centre for Planning Studies, University of Edinburgh. Licensor www.scran.ac.uk p4; Edinburgh City Libraries. Licensor www.scran.ac.uk p8; Courtesy of RCAHMS. Licensor www.rcahms.gov.uk p 9; Courtesy of Edinburgh City Archives p11; City of Edinburgh Council and www.capitalcollections.org.uk p10, p13 & p19.

Illustrations by Robert Nelmes and David Lemm. All other photography by Derek Irvine Photography.